From One Girl To Another:

Daughters of Destiny

Raelyn T. Purham

ISBN: 057841385X
ISBN-13: 978-0578413853

DEDICATION

To my Grammie,
You called me your sunshine and I will never stop shining
for you. Because of you I know how to love and care for
others. You are forever in my heart and thoughts. I love you!
Carol Ann Bonney-Parson
(1947-2007)

To my little sisters Raja and Raina,
If you all were here I would be pushing you beauties to be all
you could be. I love you and think about you both daily. Rest
in Peace my babies.
(August 27th, 2002)

CONTENTS

ACKNOWLEDGMENTS

First I would like to thank God for speaking to me while writing this entire book. Writing a book was never my plan but God's plan should always override our own. He told me exactly what I needed to say in each chapter. God wrote this book, I was simply a vessel He used. It wasn't easy, but He helped me finish strong. Thank you Dr. Robert T. Purham Jr., who is not only my father but my Pastor and Mentor as well. Thank you daddy for always believing in me, leading, and helping me every step of the way. It's because of you I know how to back up every point with scripture. Without you and your wisdom my book would be a hollow victory. I love you. Thank you to my mommy, Devlon L. Parson, for your tremendous support, encouragement, and unconditional love. Whenever I needed your assistance you were right there. Your love and the thought of how big your smile would be after I released my book carried me through. I love you cupcake! A big thanks to Ms. Kim for editing my book for me. You are the greatest and I appreciate you! Shout out to Kristen R. Harris and the "*Scribe Tribe*" for helping me push this "baby" out! Kristen you are wonderful and because of you I birthed my very first baby! Thank you to the most selfless, kind, and caring person I know, Dantrell M. Taylor. Thank you for EVERY contribution and sacrifice you've made for me and this book. The support you've shown me every single day has gone unmatched. You put in just as much time and work in as me making sure the world received every bit of greatness. You put up with a lot from me while I was getting this book together and took it all like the champ I know you are. I love you immensely. Last but not least, thank you to my siblings, Robert and Ramiah, you all are the friends I never asked for and the help I always seem to need. LOL! To my aunts, Aieshea Johnson, LaKiesha Parson, Niea Johnson, Helen Bonney, Norris Purham, Doleen Woodson, Glenda Purham, my granny, Lorine Purham, my grandfather, Dr. Donald L. Parson, my cousins, Jermoné (Jermie) Davis and Alexis (Lace) Purham, and the rest of my family, you all will always be the reasons why I follow my dreams and go hard every day. You all are watching and rooting for me, and because of your support I know I won't fail. Special thank you to Yarishia Soneé and Pint Size Couture Children's Boutique for styling all the babies for the cover photoshoot. You are amazing! Thank you to all of my supporters, readers, friends, and extended family. I love you all so much!

WALKING BY FAITH

Many of us have the gift of not looking like what we've gone through. We cover up our circumstances so well people begin to hate on us and tend to believe we have it all together strictly based on how great we look. They start to dislike and envy you because you are so nicely put together when they don't even know the story behind your appearance. If they only knew what you had to go home to or leave from, they wouldn't envy you as much. Their thoughts of you would change rather quickly. I was once the person who hid my troubles behind my outer appearance and tried to compress them to make sure nothing about my personal life seeped out. I didn't want anyone to know what was going on at home, so I made sure I looked like what I wanted people to believe…"Everything is great!"

Throughout high school, I had so many friends and of course some haters on the side too! My hair was always done. My shoes were always of the latest fashion, I was clean, and had some expensive purses and jewelry as well. My clothes were ironed, nice, and mostly name brand. I smelled good and knew I looked good every single day. My mom would tell me all the time, "You just go to school thinking it's a fashion show. You not going to learn you going to be seen." In some instances that was true, but you better believe my grades were as nice as my clothes. I knew how to manage. While many called me spoiled, no one knew the trouble I sometimes had to endure at home. My house leaked when it rained or snowed. We had buckets at the front door and in a couple of bedrooms as well. Everyone knew I had a big house, but it was only due to the fact my mother inherited it from my Grammie after she passed away. What the outsiders didn't know was that we could barely afford to maintain it. Sometimes our water would be off for a few days and maybe even a week so we washed up with water bottles my mom boiled on the stove or in the microwave. We didn't have cable and we eventually ended up losing our "great big house" due to tax issues. We later moved and it seemed as though my problems grew worse.

My parents separated my Junior year of high school and this was one problem my outer appearance just couldn't cover up. I felt as if everyone would know all of our family issues once they found out my parents were no longer together. While my siblings and I saw the separation to be necessary, I knew our friends and family didn't see it coming. I took pride in being able to say I lived in a two-parent household where me, my brother Rob, and sister Ramiah shared the same mother and father. Through every fight and storm, I still enjoyed the family bond we shared. The thought of no longer being able to say that crushed me more than I thought it would and I don't think anyone really knew that. After my parents split, my mom stopped working for a little while and we no longer could cover the house payments so we were forced to move…AGAIN! Our lights were shut off for a month and a half. We lit candles so we could have some light and bought battery powered lights to put in each room. This is what the outsiders didn't see and would've never guessed unless they decided to drop by. It wasn't noticeable and my family and I never looked like the storm that was swarming through our lives. People could have said, "Well y'all had enough to get your hair done." But I didn't go to a beauty shop. My hairdresser was my Auntie Kiesha who lived in the same house as me. I didn't have to pay her. I had nice clothes all the time because my cousin Jermie always gave me her hand-me-downs. I would sneak Kiesha's clothes all the time. Whenever I had money I bought them for myself. My shoes were Jordan's, Adidas, Nike, and all the other names because I got a job my sophomore year and racked up. Some of the shoes I wore to school I snuck from Kiesha's closet too, but no one knew unless I told them.

When I decided to volunteer private information to my friends about my life outside of school, they would barely believe me. Some even tried to trace things back like my Sweet 16 Party. Yeah, it was the Sweet 16 of my dreams, but only because I had a lot of family and friends volunteering their services to make sure I had everything I wanted. My parents were great at making me believe I could have anything I desired. I knew it wasn't easy for them to give it to me, but they still made it happen. Unfortunately for them, that didn't quite stop me from asking for a lot. Ha! For my Sweet 16 my mom paid for the candy on my candy table with food stamps, my dad paid for my venue, a friend of the family bought my cake, my Godmom bought my dress, and uncles and aunts chipped in a lot as well! To someone looking in from a crack, they would have thought I had it made. I did to a certain extent, but I still faced a lot of challenges. I must say, through every storm, my parents made sure my siblings and I ate good every single night. We have never not had a great Christmas and I always had the birthday party I wanted. No matter how over the top I was with my ideas, my parents made it happen! It's easy for outsiders to speculate based off what *they* saw, but they weren't on the inside enduring what we endured. There was a time my friends came over for a movie night I was hosting and couldn't even tell our lights were off. We had an extension cord coming from our townhouse going to our neighbor's townhouse. The T.V. and one lamp in our living room were plugged up and no one knew. There have been times where we didn't have heat so my dad would bring propane heaters to heat up the house. No matter what the circumstances were my parents always made sure we were all comfortable. We bounced from hotel to motel for a few months because we didn't have enough money to get our heat cut on one winter. No one knew that either!

See, people will judge you by your cover and not even know they could use the content you carry. They could use some of your humility and the strength you have which has caused you to allow negative opinions to roll off of you like water on a raincoat. In this life, you will be thrown so many curve balls, but don't allow anyone to take your focus off of greater. You have to walk by faith and not by sight. Where you see yourself now isn't where you will always be. I've gone through so much even outside of these issues, but I knew I wasn't going to be at the bottom forever. My head was always in the clouds even on the drowsiest days of them all. I had a royal mentality under peasant circumstances and I want you to have the same thing. I knew God had more instore for me. He wanted more for me than I could see for myself. You have to understand that same principle. Allow your present circumstances to be the motivating force behind your grind! Make major moves now so you will never have to relive your past experiences. My family is whom I grind for. They don't always act like they should or even make me feel like they know that to be true, but it doesn't matter. My actions will soon back up everything I'm saying now. My family and I have seen the worst and they deserve so much more than what they have now. God brought us through all of those situations and has put the biggest desire in my heart to be all I can for them. Start turning your negative energy into positive energy. Never let them see you sweat. Just let them see you work hard and make it to the top. It won't always be rough, but you must continue to be tough throughout the process. Only the strong can make it to the top. No weaklings allowed!

-Rae

TAKE HEED

I learned the ins and outs of relationships through observation. Every mistake I made taught me many valuable lessons and shaped me into the person I am today. We are all products of our relational experiences. It's important to learn how to appreciate your positive and negative experiences. You may not understand why you should now, but doing so will definitely help you become a better you. Every problem I have faced in life could have been avoided. Every wrong turn I have made could have been prevented if I were following directions. Following the directions of those we trust to lead us is vitally important. They help us make it to our destination just like the GPS helps us without causing us to get lost or confused.

Experience was a learning tool for me, but not the best one. It brought me unnecessary pain. It's so much easier to learn from other people's mistakes. For example, if you see when your friend puts a metal fork in the microwave, causes it to go up in flames, and it gives her third degree burns would you try doing it yourself or would you capitalize on her mistake and realize it isn't something you should do? Because you're smart, I know you would go with the second option. Obviously making a decision to put the fork in the microwave caused your friend pain, so it will cause you pain as well. That's how we have to be when it comes to life experiences. If we see one person make a mistake and get bad results why would we do the exact same thing just to get the same negative outcome? I want you to use every lesson I present to you and learn from it. I want to break the cycle of young girls making the same mistakes over and over without learning from one another. You are a *Daughter of Destiny*. It is time now for you to take direction and wisdom from those who have already experienced negative repercussions due to the bad choices they've made. *Take Heed* to the signs of "Destruction Ahead". You have too much work to do on this Earth to mess around and get caught in the devil's traps. I want you to stay ahead by learning what not to do. I wish I knew what I know now because I would have made a lot of different choices and I would not have been so stagnant. I'm giving you this information because I'm tired of seeing young girls fail and become a part of today's latest statistic. You are capable of being so much more and I want you to be so much more, but I need your help and cooperation. I need you to be alert and aware of the games the devil will try to play on you just because he wants to set you back in life. The best way to be alert and aware of the tricks of the enemy is by reading your word daily so you can clearly identify the enemy in a crowd full of people. You have to know the way he moves. It is important that you read up on how Satan tried to trap God's people in the Bible. Satan has an arsenal full of tactics to try to destroy the people of God but here is a list of just a few identifiable tactics he will try to use against you:

1.) Through Temptation (Genesis 3)
- Satan tempted Eve to eat the forbidden fruit. He tempted her with something God said was wrong to do and got her to believe God just wanted to keep a good thing to himself. That is not how God operates nor will that ever be the case because **Psalm 84:11 (NLT)** says, **"For the LORD God is our sun and our shield. He gives us grace and glory. The LORD will withhold no good thing from those who do what is right."** In other words, God will never hold out on providing you with the absolute best. Many times we hold ourselves back from having the best because we are not obedient to God and we don't cooperate with His way of doing things. Don't let that be the case for you.

2.) Through Thoughts (Genesis 3)
- Satan will attempt to get us to believe God doesn't care about us by putting the blame on God for bad things occurring in our lives. God is not the force behind anything negative happening in any of our lives. In fact, most times we cause bad things to happen to us by not being in our rightful places; or by operating outside of the will of God and by being disobedient to His Word. Satan will try to trick us into believing his lies and will try to implant them inside of our heads just so we can think twice about the goodness of God. Beware, when those doubts come rushing to your head know it's just Satan trying to throw you off course. Recognize him for the liar and deceiver he is and do not give those negative thoughts any attention.

3.) Through Attacking Your Faith (Ephesians 6:12)
- Satan is definitely one to fight against everything you believe in and because we know he will come in full force we have to be fully equipped to fight for our faith and stand up for righteousness. The stronger your faith is in God, the greater the attacks will be. That doesn't mean have little faith but it

does mean be ready to defend your faith and don't back down when it gets tough. Nothing threatens Satan more than a believer of God who has unshakeable faith. When it comes to Satan we have to be "unbothered". Trust, know, and believe in the God given power you have to knock every test out the park. We have to keep in mind that Satan is already defeated. He is not in the race to the finish line he is just on the sidelines throwing things at us to try and make us fall. Satan wants attention, he wants YOUR attention, but when you keep your attention and focus on God what he is doing to get noticed by you won't even be seen or heard. Stay focused!

4.) Through Sexual Persuasion (1 Corinthians 7:5)

- Satan doesn't want you to be pure. He will try to take that away from you by setting temptation in front of you and hoping you will grab it. You have to be strong and not let your flesh give in because this is where he has trapped many believers. After you have "done it" (had sex) one time he tricks you into thinking God no longer wants you but that is not true. God can still use you for his glorification no matter what condition you are in. Don't believe that there is no coming back from mistakes. You just have to make the decision to resist temptation until the day you become one with your spouse.

5.) Through Slander (Revelation 12:10-11)

- We have to get to a point where we realize no matter what we do some people will just never forget where we once were. That's okay because it is so easy to leave them where they are. Satan will try to use people to lay out all your sins so you can juggle them in your thoughts just so he can discredit your progress. Don't worry about it because God knows and sees you working hard and only His thoughts of you counts.

6.) Through Pride (1 Peter 5:6-8)

- Pride stops us from accessing more in the Kingdom of God. Pride is a worldly attitude not allowing us to recognize God the way He desires us to. I'm sure you can see why Satan uses us in this way. Pride is living with a blatant disregard for God and His way of doing things and Satan will use pride for his benefit just to destroy you. It's important for us to resist being self-centered and instead be God-centered. You have to get to a place where doing what God expects is a way of life and not a Plan B. When you use God as a Plan B, it creates an opportunity for Satan's plan to be Plan A.

7.) Through Things (1 John 2:15-16)

- Satan will use worldly attractions to distract us from being in daily communication with God. We should talk to God every single day because He should be the one giving us direction. How can you receive direction from God if you are not in daily communication with Him? God can't lead us if we are not following Him. In order to follow God, you have to hear the orders He is giving you. Don't allow what life has to offer to throw you off course and prevent you from receiving all God has to say to you. Satan wants us to be lost and confused. This creates an opportunity for him to lead us down the wrong path. Talking to God daily will protect you from Satan's plan.

My job is to help guide you through life and help you dodge everything avoidable. I want you to receive all the knowledge from someone like me who has been there and done it. I'm presenting my story to you so you can learn from my mistakes and get the information I wish someone had administered to me in my younger years. Together we're going to get it done! I have a story that could change the lives of so many people and I'm starting with you. I want to change your life for the better and help you redirect your steps to greater! God gave me the challenge and I'm ready to take it on!

-Rae

SET THE TONE

As women of God we should be setting the tone by being good examples to the younger generation. Living a spiritual lifestyle is far more rewarding than living a worldly lifestyle. Many of us have the misconception of believing great things come out of living life in the fast lane. That's not necessarily true. Living in the fast lane can cut your life short. Why do you think it is more common for a person who is speeding to get into a car accident than one who isn't speeding? When you speed through life you can miss the signs designed to protect you from collision. Slow down and take precaution.

We sometimes make the mistake of trying to blend in with those around us. We often try to mix our identity with those we are supposed to be set apart from which causes us to lose ourselves. That was once my mindset. I had to make a conscious decision to live a spiritual lifestyle and one that would please the God I told everyone I served.

Romans 12:2 (KJV)

"And be not conformed to this world: but be ye transformed by the renewing of your mind, that ye may prove what is good, and acceptable, and perfect, will of God."

I was once the child who could not get it together. I was acting up in school, hanging with the wrong crowd, and very rebellious. I wanted to do right but I couldn't. I reminded myself of Paul in the book of Romans.

Romans 7:19 (NLT)

"I want to do what is good, but I don't. I don't want to do what is wrong, but I do it anyway."

My heart was in the right place and I knew it because I felt convicted every time I did something wrong. In this life, we have to be in the world without allowing it to influence our decision-making. We are not natural beings but spiritual beings who have to learn to be examples to those looking up to us. We sometimes have the wrong thinking when it comes to things like how we should dress when going to church. I often hear the worn out excuse, "God says come as you are". First, the bible doesn't say that and secondly, what happens after you've pressed your way to come to church, heard the word, and learned what is and is not acceptable? Shouldn't there be some changes made? Everyone likes being able to wear what they want and shouldn't feel as if their outside appearance interferes with them being a pure hearted individual and true worshipper of Christ. What you wear to church doesn't change those things, but it does cause others to perceive you differently. I hope you know it doesn't matter what people think about you, however in the body of Christ it is our job to make sure we represent God to the best of our ability.

1 Corinthians 8:13 (NLT)

"If what I eat causes another believer to sin, I will never eat meat again as long as I live—for I don't want to cause another believer to stumble."

In other words, if you are doing something that causes another believer to want to sin you should rethink and refrain. In the natural, having lustful thoughts about the young lady in the short skirt or tight dress can lead to judgement of the young lady. As the body of Christ, it is our job to ensure the focus stays on God while in church. We shouldn't allow the natural realm to effect what is going on spiritually.

For example, it's your first time going to church and the short tight dress in your closet is all you have but you really want to go; you should still go because God definitely knows your heart and will see its purity. Because your heart is in the right place, someone may randomly bless you with something more suitable along the way. God will make provisions for you in an instant because He recognizes a need and never falls short on meeting the need for His children. The conflict only comes in when you have more appropriate outfits but you just choose the one that is undoubtedly inappropriate for church. If you decide to wear it you may end up upset or uncomfortable when someone says something to you about it being inappropriate. Correction is always in order as long as it is done in love, with tact, and respect. We have to be receptive to correction and respectful to the order in which things are supposed to be done. We cannot continue to do things the way we want to just because we feel like it. Why? Because it causes our other brothers and sisters in Christ to stumble just like

1 Corinthians 8:13 says.

Galatians 6:1 (NLT)

"Dear brothers and sisters, if another believer is overcome by some sin, you who are godly should gently and humbly help that person back onto the right path. And be careful not to fall into the same temptation yourself."

2 Timothy 4:2 (NLT)

"Preach the word of God. Be prepared, whether the time is favorable or not. Patiently correct, rebuke, and encourage your people with good teaching."

As believers of God we have to choose to be better examples and representations of Christ. The benefits of living a life which honors God is so much more rewarding than what the people on this Earth could ever give to us. Living a life pleasing to God is a life worth living because it ensures not only your safety on this Earth but your character as well. As a woman of God, you have an image to uphold and it does not include being half naked in the streets or getting wasted at a club. Asking yourself, "How does this glorify God?" should become a focus. The more you focus on God the more you will change. Your God-focus will change your priorities because we don't glorify God in the club.

Your understanding will increase when making the switch from worldly to spiritual and your interest will change. You could have been a fan of parties and going out all the time, but now since you have been fulfilled through Christ, the only thing you want to do is go to church and praise God. It can and will get to a point where you get so high off of living a Godly lifestyle, your desires begin to change. What you once wanted to wear and be seen out in is something you no longer choose. Where you once wanted to go is no longer appealing. The liquor you once wanted to drink isn't even attractive like it was before. God has a way of changing how we view things when we give Him all of us and bask in His presence daily. The things you once saw a need for will no longer have a place in your life. You thought smoking and drinking took your mind off of things but later realized God can release you from all of those things forever. The feeling of being totally free from the cares of the world can only be given by God. There is liberation in Him!

It's time for you to make the transition from the natural into the spiritual and rest there forever. There is no room for you to blend and go with the flow. You have to set the tone for the next generation and let the world see that life with Jesus is so much better than life without Him. I'm not saying you have to stop listening to Beyoncé, J Cole, Lil Herb, or BJ the Chicago Kid, but just don't forget who you are while listening to them. Be so confident to the point you can listen to worldly music and be unaffected by it. It's fine to celebrate things and have fun with friends, but do it while still honoring God. You do not have to be the one drunk, puking, or standing on tables twerking. Be mindful of the fact God sees everything you do. If you don't mind God seeing you in that way, then so be it, but if you wouldn't want your parents seeing it then it's definitely something God shouldn't see you doing either. Standards should change. The new normal shall be the norm.

With that being said, as a Woman of God, you have to be mindful of what is appropriate and inappropriate so we will not wrongly influence others. One of the greatest things you have in this world and you should not want to taint is <u>your character</u>. Respect yourself and the God you serve.

-*Rae*

LIVING BY THE WORD

It's easy to love someone who loves you but the test comes when you have to love someone you have so much anger towards. I've failed this test many times but eventually had to get it right. As believers of God, we have a responsibility to be doers of the Word of God no matter the situation.

Luke 6:31 (NCV)

"Do to others what you would want them to do to you."

As Christians, this is our daily assignment simply because God said it. We cannot pick and choose what rules we want to follow and which ones we don't. God doesn't choose which sins He will forgive and which ones He won't. He sent Jesus to die for all of them so all are forgiven for believers of God. It means, simply, when one of our family members or friends do wrong by us, we still have a duty to do right by them and love them in spite of their wrong. I'm not saying it's an easy task, but dying on the cross for the sins of others could not have been easy either, however, we can still say mission accomplished. Can God say that about you when it comes to you doing what you're supposed to do? You may be saying it is easier said than done but here you have someone saying it who in fact really had to do it, and can now count it as a mission accomplished. I was tested in this area a while back. God literally spoke to me and said the exact words I started this chapter off with. I had to think about it because as a natural being, things like that aren't easy to do. I had a few people in my life lie on me, drag my name through the mud, hurt me, talk about me, envy me, and God wanted me to love and forgive them even still. I understood why but for some reason it didn't make me want to do it. In order for God to forgive us we have to forgive others who have wronged us. They could be family members, friends, sisters, brothers, abusers, attackers, killers, rapists, and so on. No matter what, God wants us to forgive and love them even still. It doesn't mean they have to be in your face 24/7 or even allowed in your space. As long as you have forgiven them and still love them, you are in good standing with God.

For most Christians, the struggle is not believing in God or in the power He possesses, but it is adhering to His Word and doing what it says. Believing in the Lord and Savior gets you to heaven but abiding by His word and being obedient gains you access to the blessings and promises of God. Did you know the blessing is already yours? It's just waiting for you to position yourself in alignment with the will of God so you can receive it. God rewards faithfulness and His rewards come in many forms.

Leviticus 26:3-4 (NCV)

"If you remember my laws and commands and obey them, I will give you rains at the right season; the land will produce crops, and the trees of the field will produce their fruit."

Leviticus 26:6-7 (NCV)

"I will give you peace to your country; you will lie down in peace, and no one will make you afraid. I will keep harmful animals out of your country, and armies will not pass through it. You will chase your enemies and defeat them, killing them with your sword."

Leviticus 26:9 (NCV)

"Then I will show kindness to you and let you have many children; I will keep my agreement with you."

In essence, nothing you do for God goes unrewarded. It is time now for you to up your commitment to Him. You can't say you want to please God but deliberately disobey His word. Fill the holes in your commitment to God and take the hold off of your blessings by fully committing to obey everything His Word says. This one task will open so many doors and cause an overflow of blessings, prosperity, and good things to happen in your life. It's time to flourish on Earth and that requires a huge commitment. Now is the time to let go of the hurt others caused you and forgive!

-Rae

WATCH YOUR MOUTH

As believers of God and people with a purpose, we have to pay close attention to what we permit to come out of our mouths. You should never want to put any negativity into the atmosphere. Have you noticed, the things we speak have a tendency to come to life. What comes out of your mouth determines what comes into your life.

Proverbs 18:21 (KJV)

"Death and life are in the power of the tongue: and they that love it shall eat the fruit thereof."

It is imperative we focus all of our energy on positive things. We must be conscious about the things we say, even when joking. We must be mindful of everything we say in every way.

Ephesians 4:29 (KJV)

"Let no corrupt communication proceed out of your mouth, but that which is good to the use of edifying, that it may minister grace unto the hearers."

Many of us fail to remember the undeniable power our words have. Words can either cause your life to flourish or cause it to destruct. The word of God confirms it for us in numerous scriptures. While getting your life, mind, and relationships in order you have to remember to guard your mouth and truly think before you speak.

You now have to learn how to speak less about negative situations and speak more power over them to see change. When you wake up in the morning start speaking life into your day. Here are a few examples:

"Job you will give me life today!"

"I will live and not die!"

"My life is getting better each and every day!"

"This homework is easy and not hard!"

You have the power to control everything around you. In order for change to occur, you have to see it and believe it in your heart and mind first. When you speak positively you begin to see positivity around you. You may not believe what you say at first, but once you start speaking things into existence, it will feel so good to the point you have no choice but to believe it. It is a simple task which has not been taken advantage of by the body of Christ. Now is your time to use it and watch it work for you in your life.

-*Rae*

RECOGNIZING YOU

You cannot learn someone else when you barely know anything about yourself. When I say someone else, I'm referencing individuals you desire to be in relationship with, the people around you, or those you are already connected to. You can also apply this to the person you are in a relationship with right now, if you are in fact in a relationship now. How can you learn the people around you without first knowing who you are? I am not referencing your personal desires, wants, likes or dislikes right now. This time I want you to go below the surface and figure out who God says you are by searching through the word of God. The Bible has countless scriptures that tell us exactly who we are. You should use them to help shape your natural identity.

Knowing who you are spiritually will cause you to live and operate on a different level naturally. I'm going to share a few scriptures with you referencing your identity in Christ. You should apply each and every one of these scriptures to yourself and remind yourself of them daily. Write them down and tape them all over your room/house so you will never forget who God created you to be.

If You Have Given Your Life to Christ You Are…

John 15:15

- a friend of Jesus

Roman 3:24

- justified and redeemed

John 1:12

- a child of God

Romans 8:1

-Free from condemnation

Romans 8:2

-Free from the law of sin and death

Romans 8:17

-a fellow heir with Christ

1 Corinthians 1:30

-One who has wisdom, righteousness, sanctification, and redemption

1 Corinthians 6:19

-One whose body is a temple of the Holy Spirit who dwells in you

1 Corinthians 6:17

-Joined to the Lord and one spirit with Him

2 Corinthians 2:14

-One who God leads in triumph and knowledge of Christ

2 Corinthians 5:17

-New creature in Christ

Galatians 5:1

-Been set free in Christ

Ephesians 1:3

-Blessed with every spiritual blessing in the heavenly places

Ephesians 1:4

-Chosen, holy, and blameless before God

Ephesians 1:7

-Redeemed and forgiven by the grace of Christ

Ephesians 1:11

-Predestined by God to obtain an inheritance

Ephesians 2:4-5

-Been made alive with Christ

Ephesians 2:6

-Seated in heavenly places with Christ

Ephesians 2:10

-God's workmanship created to produce good works

Ephesians 3:6

-Partner of Christ's promise

Ephesians 5:8

-Light in the Lord

Philippians 3:20

-Citizen of Heaven

Philippians 4:19

-supplied with every need

Colossians 2:10

-Complete in Christ

1 Peter 2:9

-Royal Priesthood

2 Timothy 1:7

-Without fear

1 Corinthians 6:20

-Bought with a price

Psalm 139:14

-Wonderfully Made

Philippians 4:13

-Limitless

These are just a few scripture references that put us in remembrance of who God created us to be on Earth, how He views us, and also how we should view ourselves. I bet you didn't know you were all of these things. It is important for us to get a right understanding concerning who we are spiritually in this natural world before we get to know someone else. Before I acquired this understanding and knowledge I prayed for these things without knowing they were already mine. I prayed to be fearless not knowing God made me fearless. The world conditioned me to believe fear had to exist in my life in order to be human, but that isn't how God intended for me or you to live. We must stop allowing the world to dictate who we are because the world took no part in creating us. Learn who you are from the person who created you. The world can only teach us what can be proven through study and research. God's way of doing things is by making the impossible possible. His moves are different from ours and often inexplicable but definitely appreciated.

While going in the world, keep in mind who you are from a biblical standpoint and do not leave any room for uncertainty.

Psalm 139:14 (NLT)

"Thank you for making me so wonderfully complex! Your workmanship is marvelous—how well I know it."

-Rae

MAKING THE DIFFERENCE

Let's walk through the streets of reality for a few moments. We live in a generation where girls think having a smart mouth is cute and having a baby at a young age while unmarried is celebrated. It's treated like it is a major accomplishment. We live in a world where respect is not given to elders and authority is almost always questioned. We're in a world where getting the latest Jordan's is more important than obtaining a degree. As young ladies, we feel forced to grow up and because the only examples we tend to look to are girls like Kylie Jenner, Kim Kardashian, and Amber Rose; We are all confused. Girls who are 15 look like they are 20, sex is selling more than books, and our prisons are more populated with African Americans more than colleges and universities. It is time for us to do better and we have to start with ourselves, the man in the mirror, or shall I say girl. I need your help to change the rhythm of the beat. In order to help someone else change you have to be an example of change. The first step is changing your mentality. The one thing that can change everything is your thinking. The way you think affects how you live. Having a negative attitude and a smart mouth all the time will not get you anywhere, or shall I say it won't get you far. Only a person with a child-like mindset believes throwing tantrums will get them what they want. Real adults don't even try it because they know that doesn't really work!

We should always want to live in positivity and have a reputable background and solid character. Society often puts a stamp of approval on a lot of things considered wrong to God. I, personally, do not believe in celebrating an unmarried expecting mother especially if she is still in high school. This kind of thing does not deserve a celebration. It should receive reprimanding and rebuking because it is imperative that she understands why it is wrong and unacceptable. I only feel that way because it is out of the order in which God established for us to do things.

1 Corinthians 6:18 (MSG)

"There is a sense in which sexual sins are different from all others. In sexual sin we violate the sacredness of our own bodies, these bodies that were made for God-given and God-molded love, for "becoming one" with another."

1 Thessalonians 4:3 (NLT)

"God's will is for you to be holy, so stay away from sexual sin."

Colossians 3:5 (MSG)

"And that means killing off everything connected with that way of death: sexual promiscuity, impurity, lust, doing whatever you feel like whenever you feel like it, and grabbing whatever attracts your fancy. That's a life shaped by things instead of by God."

Why celebrate being outside of God's will? Having a baby out of wedlock is unworthy of a celebration simply because it isn't in alignment with the word of God. In cases like this, we fail to recognize where the mistake is being made which then causes us to continue to make the same mistake because we never learned from the unidentified mistake. This is not to say that if you did have a baby before marriage you are destined for hell, but now that you know what is right in the sight of God use it to bounce back. Don't close the book yet. There is hope for every story you may have and even if you've made a mistake along the way. There is still a light at the end of the tunnel to show you the way out of what may look like darkness. I'm not pure. I've made mistakes on my journey, but I took it and used it as a learning tool. I used to beat myself up about it because I knew God didn't want me to be out of order but then God put me in remembrance of something called grace. He forgave me and didn't hold my sin against me. He showed me free and unmerited favor and unconditional love even in my unclean state. That's what lead me to brush myself off and live a life that was holy and acceptable to Christ. His love drew me back to Him. In order to learn from your mistake, you must first <u>recognize</u> the mistake when you see or make one.

It seems like we are so quick to impress people with material things but tend to be unimpressive in the areas that truly count. It's kind of like being a pretty girl without having the brains, substance, and good character to match. We'd rather have the latest clothes, make-up, and jewelry while only being able to maintain a C or D average in school. We'd rather take the time to look nice at school or at the parties and then go to church ready to say, "He said come as you are." This is what I mean when I say we must change our way of thinking. We have to make sure first things are first. Our priorities must be in alignment. Prioritizing should put God in the #1 position where He always belongs. Society has us believing looking nice is more important than being smart. Having a nice body is better than having an education. We think things like speaking improperly is cute and it's not. Having an education and obtaining a degree will get you further than having a nice body ever will. You need brains to make it in this world. If you don't have proper knowledge, you'll fall for anything. If you fall for anything you will always find yourself on the ground. My daddy always told me not to go with the flow. Create your own flow. Everyone wants success, fame, and wealth but no one wants to put in the work to get it. Everyone is looking for a get rich quick scheme, but no one wants to look for a job. Everyone wants to ride the wave, but who is learning how to surfboard so they don't get wiped out? This is one of the laziest generations this world has ever seen and quite frankly it's sad. We have to switch it up and start making a difference in the world.

Proverbs 10:4 (NLT)

"Lazy people are soon very poor; hard workers get rich."

Being lazy is unacceptable, further your education and be wise in your decision making so you can build an empire. My job is not to tear you down but to redirect you in a positive direction and help you identify the areas in your life that need a little more assistance. Before one can give direction one has to learn how to take direction. There are enough people in this world who see our youth going downhill and not doing anything about it. I want the body of Christ to do better, live better, and be the best simply because it's the will of God. You have to make the difference and be the change we need so that things can be in order. There are plenty of opportunities out here ready for you to grab. Stop settling for mediocre garbage and be all that you can be and then some. There is greatness inside of you so tap into it and start living blessed.

-Rae

THE WINNER'S CIRCLE

2 Corinthians 6:14 (NLT)

"Don't team up with those who are unbelievers. How can righteousness be a partner with wickedness? How can light live with darkness?"

1 Corinthians 15:33 (MSG)

"But don't fool yourselves. Don't let yourselves be poisoned by this anti-resurrection loose talk. "Bad company ruins good manners."

Surrounding yourself with individuals who have the heart to please God just as much as you do is very important. You should want people around you who will pour into you and add to your greatness. Avoid those who do not value you, appreciate you, or agree with the direction you are heading in. The relationships you choose will either add to or take away from your righteous commitment.

Throughout high school, I had a core group of friends who I could bring to church, talk about church with, pray with, shout with, cry with, and worship God in front of them without feeling any embarrassment. Those are the kind of people you need in your life. You need individuals who will not look at you funny because you want to please God and do the right thing. You need friends who do not mind praying with you about whatever you need them to. You also need friends who will hold you accountable when you get of track. People like that are God-sent. Those types of people encourage and help you stay on the right track.

Everyone around you should be going up just like you. When you have people around you who are doing well, succeeding, and prospering it is harder to fall off than it would be if you had people who were the complete opposite. When you see your friends reaching for the stars it makes you want to reach for them as well. A person without a plan for their own life can't add anything valuable to yours. They are simply dead weight. Smother yourself with winners who will show you and help you put your plans into action so you can be a winner too.

This lesson can be a hard one to catch on to only because it forces you to reevaluate a few of your friendships. But, if you are serious about winning in life, you must be serious about cutting a few people off who do not have your best interest. You know who genuinely wants to see you go higher based on how they respond to your victories. The one who gets excited for you like it is them who just experienced something great is the one you need to keep in your corner. You need people around who express an unfeigned interest in your success. A real friend is one who can truly be happy for your success even if it does not include them getting something out of it. Real friends should want the people around them to be on their level or higher. Those are the ones who do not allow jealousy to take over their thoughts and emotions and cause them to secretly hurt or demise you. Keep individuals around who you can talk to and those you know won't go running off to the next person sharing all your business with them. People like that are not real friends they're simply imposters. Some people are only around you to make sure you aren't ahead of them and to keep tabs on you. Get rid of those kind of people. They are just taking up the space a true supporter could have. Sometimes the best friends out there are family members and sometimes the best ones aren't.

Proverbs 18:24 (MSG)

"Friends come and go, but a true friend sticks by you like family."

Proverbs 13:20 (MSG)

"Become wise by walking with the wise; hang out with fools and watch your life fall to pieces."

Go evaluate and pray over your friendships. Sometimes we make the mistake of thinking someone has pure intentions regarding us when really, they had a malicious intent the whole time. Ask God to reveal and remove those who were not sent by Him and praise Him for the ones who have been.

-*Rae*

GROWTH WITHOUT A STORM

Behind every anointed individual is a testimony that helped them tap into their anointing. There is growth in every failure only if you learn. When we fail, we have to be open minded enough to see where we messed up and how we steered ourselves in the wrong direction. Being hardheaded, stubborn, and believing everything we do is right is what causes us to fall. We usually don't realize why it is important for us to get up until we are on the ground. It's so easy to stay down and forget how we got there. We have to redirect our attention to why we fell and now why we have to get up and get it right.

Many people believe it is God who knocks us down just so we can look up to Him for help. but that is untrue. God is a God of order so He will not cause disorder just to get you in order. God isn't going to put you through hell just to teach you a lesson. Instead He capitalizes on what people bring on themselves.

1 Corinthians 14:33 (NLT)

"For God is not a God of disorder but of peace, as in all the meetings of God's holy people."

We are the products of our own mistakes. When we fall and fail it is often because we pushed ourselves down, not because God was teaching us a lesson. God taught us our lessons in the Bible. It is up to us to read, listen, and follow it to stay on track and on our feet. Once you take God's word for face value, then you will have less room for errors and mistakes. We have the word of God as a guide so we do not have to experience the failures and disappointments the rest of the world is experiencing. The word of God is the key to our results not the storms of life. If you need a storm to teach you a lesson you have not really found value in the word of God.

Our trials, tribulations, and negative circumstances help us learn and better ourselves. You do not need those things to grow. You do not stunt your growth by not making mistakes. You can and should learn and benefit from the experiences of others.

Not listening to God caused so many people to hurt themselves and you can find those lessons in the Bible. You don't have to test the truth of what happens when you don't listen to God to know that it is going to land you on your back. You can get that understanding through the Word of God. We punish ourselves by not listening and obeying God's word. Just like in the book of Genesis chapter 19, God sent angels to tell Lot and his wife the city he lived in was going to be burned down so he needed to run to the mountains and not look back. Lot did not obey the angels and his wife looked back and was turned into a pillar of salt. Because of Lot's disobedience he lost his wife and his 2 daughters made bad choices later on in life. The point is, a split second decision can have a long-lasting effect on your life. Life throws us many curve balls, but you have to understand that we are not meant to hit them. We try hitting them every time and the ball doesn't go anywhere. We cause ourselves to lose the game simply by taking the bat from God. He wants to hit our curve balls out the park but we are too busy thinking we can grand slam them better than He can.

Psalms 55:22 (NIV)

"Cast your cares on the Lord and he will sustain you; he will never let the righteous be shaken."

Psalms 55:22 (NLT)

"Give your burdens to the Lord, and he will take care of you. He will not permit the godly to slip and fall."

God wants all of your problems, heavy loads, and burdens. Trust Him with them so you can live freely and to the full effect in which God intended you to live. We all have been anointed to do something, but don't go fooling with problems and issues just to realize it. You have enough testimonies under your belt to help someone else. Be a blessing by teaching someone else a lesson so they won't have to experience all that you did. Grow in the Lord and not in the rain.

-*Rae*

IT'S ALL AN ACT

Genesis 1:27 (NIV)

"So God created mankind in his own image, in the image of God he created them; male and female he created them."

God has created us in His image, yet we do not look nor act anything like Him. We are no longer recognizable. We have done exactly what God told us not to do and haven't done anything He said do.

Romans 12:2 (KJV)

"And be not conformed to this world: but be ye transformed by the renewing of your mind, that ye may prove what <u>IS</u> that good, and acceptable, and perfect, will of God."

We have conformed to this world and have lost our true identities. We have turned our backs to God and opened our arms up to receive the devil and adapt to his ways and have called it right. We have become careless in our thinking, speaking, and actions. We don't represent God. We disown Him just to find worldly justification for our foolery. The church is being mocked and its sanctity has been diluted due to us trying to convert to the beliefs of the world rather than sticking to the Word of God. We have all been casted in the devil's book of confusion. We have become characters in the world's play and have thrown out the truth (Bible) and called it fake. We have become stuck in this natural way of order that we no longer remember whose we are or who we are supposed to represent. We have not separated ourselves like we were told to do, instead we are part of the conglomerate confused individuals when we should be apart from it.

We have become Christians who don't want division between the world and the church but forgot that we are supposed to be divisible, differentiated, and set apart from the world. There are too many saints with sinner's problems simply because the saints are too busy thinking like sinners.

If we, the church, continue to look and act like the world, how can the world come to the church for leadership, guidance, or assistance when they face worldly issues? It's time for you to change your garments of confusion in for garments of leadership and wisdom and begin to renew your mind. We have been the devil's puppets for far too long. He has confused so many of us and it is time for us to take our lives back and place them back in the hands of the rightful owner, God! I challenge you to be yourself in the spiritual realm. Be who God called you to be. Let the world see and notice the God within you in all you do. Don't dim your light, turn it up a notch and let the glory of God shine through you each and every day!

-*Rae*

PRAYER WORKS

If you don't have a prayer life by now it is definitely past time for you to get one. The power of prayer is so undeniably strong. When we are consistent with our prayer life and serious about God He will consistently bless us in serious ways. We cannot half do God. If you don't want only half of your prayers answered don't half praise God, half worship God, or be only half serious about God. He wants all of us on a consistent basis, not just when we feel like it or when we need a mighty move of God. He wants us even if there's nothing wrong. One of the best things about God is that it is never all or nothing with Him. Whether we give Him all of us or not we will still always have full access to Him. If you give some He will give some, but if you give all you have He will give you all you want and all you've been missing. I know because I have experienced it.

I prayed to God about many things on countless occasions but it was only when my walk became serious and I started focusing on God that things began to change for the better. It seemed like every time I went to church I got confirmation regarding the prayer I prayed the night before. It felt as if the sermon preached was tailored just for me. Very rarely did the message not hit home. The confirmations were set up in ways where I was able to recognize that I was one step closer than I was before. Every sermon was designed to teach and prepare me for higher.

It would do me no good if God just answered my prayers right out the gate without me being ready to receive it. A preparation was necessary. When you get on a plane, before you take off, the flight attendant comes in and talks for a while. She isn't talking to waste time, but more so to provide you with specific instructions on what to do in case of an emergency. The flight attendant's job is to make sure you are aware of every procedure and protocol. She wants to make sure you are prepared to survive in the case of any unfortunate occurrence. If you want to go higher, you must know what to do when the enemy wants to attack you because of your ALTITUDE. When the enemy tries to come for you do not allow him to change your ATTITUDE. Like the flight attendant says, "remain calm". Because you are aware of the procedure, you know everything will be alright. Do not be afraid for God is with you. God brought you up so trust Him to bring you out and guide you through any turbulence you may experience while in the air.

Next time you pray, pray with power. Pray with authority, might, and faith because everything will be all right. I dare you to pray your dreams become reality. Pray that you reach your full potential and that your eyes be opened up to everything they were blind to. Pray God opens your ears so you can hear His voice clearly. Pray your family members be saved, all debt is canceled, and every sickness in your body is already healed. Pray without limitations or restraints. Pray your wildest prayer and watch what God does for you.

Isaiah 7:11 (MSG)

"Ask for a sign from your God. Ask anything. Be extravagant. Ask for the moon!"

Don't play with God. He said ask and you shall receive. That's one of the benefits of being a Child of God. Nothing is off-limits. Use your power and tap into the "I Amness" of God. There are some things you don't even have to pray for but you do have to speak it, declare it, decree it, and put a praise on it as you count it as being done. God is what He does. He heals so He is a Healer. He delivers so He is a Deliverer. He provides so he is a Provider. He saves so He is a Savior. He makes a way so He is a Way-Maker. He comforts us in the time of need so He is a Comforter. He is a Counselor, Sustainer, Redeemer, the Great I am, Lawyer, and a Keeper. Tap into who He is and never forget it.

Remembering and believing who God is will cause you to have more testimonies than you can imagine. Most things you've been praying for have already been answered. Things like healing, chains being broken, and sins being forgiven were all administered to believers of Christ when Jesus died on the cross.

Do not keep praying for battles you have already won. Ask God to help you believe and increase your faith in those areas. Open your Word and read! Prayer works and I'm a living witness. Get to praying, professing, and believing so you can start seeing your prayers be answered.

-*Rae*

IT'S ALREADY YOURS

God is very organized, detailed, and never misses the mark. With that being said, there is no room for confusion in anything He is a part of. God is very clear with His promises and plans He has for our lives. It is up to you to follow Him and not just incorporate Him in your life but make Him the Head of Your Life and His word the Guide for Your Life. God already has every situation worked out for you. A divine outcome has already been scheduled concerning what you face and it is in your favor.

Romans 8:28 (NLT)

"And we know that God causes everything to work together for the good of those who love God and are called according to his purpose for them."

God is not making any last minute changes to the plans He has for our lives but they cannot go into full effect until we are in full agreement with Him and His Word. Every problem you face has already been defeated. You must believe it wholeheartedly and trust God to see it. Stop trying to fight battles already won. Victory isn't something we as believers have to go after, victory has already been given to us.

Ephesians 1:3 (NLT)

"All praise to God, the Father of our Lord Jesus Christ, who has blessed us with every spiritual blessing in heavenly realms because we are united with Christ."

You have already been set up by God for inevitable success. With God, you cannot fail because in Him there is no failure. Due to you being an Heir to the Kingdom of God the only failure you may experience would only be because of your lack of following the plan God created for you. Say goodbye to your will and let God's will be done in your life.

Ephesians 2:5-6 (NLT)

"That even though we were dead because of our sins, he gave us life when he raised Christ from the dead. (It is only by God's grace that you have been saved!) For he raised us from the dead along with Christ and seated us with him in heavenly realms because we are united with Christ Jesus."

People do not understand they hurt themselves by not following the lead of God. You may sometimes think your plan will get you to your desired destination faster, but in reality, it only delays you and puts you further behind where God intended for you to be. God's plan has not been put together at the last minute or spur the moment. It was thought out and foreseen which is something many of us fail to realize. Every move you make without God pushes your destiny and the blessings God has for you back more and more. Do not delay yourself any longer. It's time for you to go get your stuff!

-Rae

DOUBLE FOR YOUR TROUBLE

There was a time when my family was moving and we were required to put our things in a storage unit until it was time for us to move into our new place of residence. The day finally came and we were only able to get a few things out of storage because our car wasn't large enough to fit everything. We moved all we could when going into our new place and never went back for the rest of our things in the storage unit. Prior to this experience, my mom went through something similar in her younger years but this wasn't something I was familiar with at all. She called the storage place one time to get the total cost of what she had to pay to get the rest of the items out of storage but never got them. A few months later, I just so happened to stumble across a letter from the storage facility and called to see if they still had our items and the man said no. He did not offer any explanation, reason, or location of where everything had gone, he just gave me a flat out no. I'll never forget the way he said it because I was so appalled at how he was just so nonchalant about our things. Like I said before, I was devastated. I lost my prom dress, clothes, shoes, and I'm sure a few more things that I just can't recall. I was so upset with my mother because I felt like no real effort was put forth to get those items back. These were things that meant something to me and things I worked to buy for myself. When I got my first job I made a promise to myself that with my first check, I would buy myself a pair of really expensive shoes that my parents wouldn't purchase. That particular pair of shoes was in the storage unit as well. The shoes I worked for. The ones I planned on keeping just to remind myself of my first check, first job, first real expensive purchase I made on myself and for it to just be taken from me hurt me. People say material things don't matter but they do when great memories are attached to them from moments you just can't relive. We lost things that my Grammie personally asked me to hold on to and cherish and so much more. It really hurt and I just felt robbed of what was MINE. No one seemed to care as much as I did either, which kind of bugged me out too. What people don't seem to realize is this, some material things have a way of reminding you where you once were. Once you lose that you have nothing left to show for it.

In the midst of my anger, hurt, and aggravation I knew there was something good I could take out of this horrible experience. When you have to deal with situations which are out of your control the best thing for you to do is pray and begin to ask God to comfort you and fill the void in your life. It will only be difficult if you keep allowing the devil to enter into your thoughts and make you upset over and over again. Ask God to help you forgive those who you thought had more control of the situation than you did and who could have blocked it from happening but didn't try hard enough to prevent it. You may not understand why, but you have to continue to move forward. We are faced with challenges all the time. We must not let them bring us down or keep us at a low state of mind. You have to use situations like this as motivation to go after your dreams and desires to make you wealthy enough to never have to face a situation like this again. As I was praying I heard God say to me, "What you lost in storage will not compare to what you will gain in the future!" That was definitely something I could rejoice about and so can you. Your storage could be completely different from mine. It doesn't have to be an actual storage unit. It could be an old house, car, or any place where you have lost something valuable or meaningful to you. What you lost doesn't have to be clothes, shoes, or anything tangible. It could be a place where you lost your sense of security, stability, peace of mind, or your virginity because someone took it from you. Whatever your storage is and whatever you lost in it can be restored by God to the point where you will never feel the emptiness again. God can fill the voids and because you endured, kept moving forward, and pushed through, He is going to reward you in the best way possible. He sees you crying and hurting over things out of your control. God hasn't forgotten about you.

Psalms 56:8 (NLT)

"You keep track of all my sorrows. You have collected all my tears in your bottle. You have recorded each one in your book."

Don't let whatever you are dealing with break you. It may hurt right now, but God always has a way of making bad situations better. Keep the faith and stay in the fight. You're up next to win! It's your turn! You are a Daughter of Destiny!

-Rae

BE PATIENT

Good things come to those who wait… Just when you think it is time to throw in the towel God steps in with a blessing up His sleeve. God never fails and is always on time. He hears your prayers and knows what your heart desires. If you are patient and obedient to His Word He will give you everything you need and long for.

I love how God operates. His way of doing things is like no other. We know what we want but God knows what we need. Sometimes what we need doesn't look as good as what we want but He has a way of making it appealing to the eye and wonderful for the heart. God hears you praying for the kind of guy you want and hears all the qualities, characteristics, and attributes you want him to have. The key to getting him is being patient and not rushing the process. When you are connected with God what you need will turn out to be everything you have ever wanted. It's almost like magic but better because it's real.

Some of the greatest blessings come at the most unexpected moments in our lives. I'm a witness! We tend to look for great things in all the wrong places. When you become spiritually in tune, you will realize that some things are not for you to look for. Such as a man. You are supposed to wait for him to find you. We mess up by searching and thinking we found a treasure when really we found a rock wrapped up in foil. The right man will find you at the right time and it will be hard to see anything bad about the chosen one. Do not give up, do not lose your faith, keep praying, and trusting God's plan for your life. Everything will be just fine. You are someone's Good Thing and the chosen one will recognize you. Your day is coming sooner than you think. Hold on to the word of God and remember His promises to you. He won't fail you.

-Rae

INTERCESSORY

in·ter·ces·sor (noun)- a person who intervenes on behalf of another, especially by prayer.

We all have family members who we would love to see make it, but they struggle internally. Those things could range from a struggle with sin or possibly a generational curse that has them bound. You see the potential in them to do great things but they can't keep their foot out of mess long enough to tap into their own abilities. This particular person could go to church every Sunday but someway and somehow get off track by the time they return home.

You've waited to see the greatness inside of them be exposed, but they can't get a grip long enough to make things happen for themselves. If they don't bust a move you have to by going to war in prayer on their behalf. Drop everything and pray that their blind eyes be uncovered, deaf ears be opened, and decree and declare that they will be delivered from all evil and be all God created them to be. Pray for their purpose to be revealed to them and fulfilled in this life. Pray against everything that is hindering them and holding them back from being great. Pray they gain clarity, sight, and a renewed mind. God gave you the power to take back everything and everyone the devil has stolen. Pray for them without ceasing. Pray and expect results. **(P)ray (U)ntil (S)omething (H)appens!** You have to go in for them and give everything you have and not hold back. It's got to happen. God will bring them over! Use your power and authority.

If they won't pray for themselves, you do it. Pray God increases their desire to want to be in good standing with Him. He will do it for His glory! After you pray rejoice and thank God every time for making it happen. Let the devil know you are a force to be reckoned with. You alone can save your entire family. Little prayer equals little power; no prayer equals no power.

Jude 1:24-25 (KJV)

"Now unto him that is able to keep you from falling, and to present you faultless before the presence of his glory with exceeding joy, to the only wise God our Saviour, be glory and majesty, dominion and power, both now and forever. Amen."

God can make things better if you hand everything over to Him. Give Him total control to change things. It will work out for you. Once you start seeing what you prayed for just open your mouth and bless God then repeat the cycle. Preach it until you reach it. People do not understand the power of prayer because they never used it when they really needed to only when they wanted to. Don't be that person. Use the tool during the good, bad, hard, and easiest times. Your words have power. Everything is getting ready to change for you. If you don't know what to say just pray and come against everything you see is wrong. Pray the desire to feed your flesh is replaced with the desire to please God in everything you do. Be confident in the fact that your prayers will change things.

James 5:16 (NIV)

"Therefore confess your sins to each other and pray for each other so that you may be healed, the prayer of a righteous person is powerful and effective."

-*Rae*

EXITING THE STORM

There may have been a time in your life where you felt like you were all out of encouragement to give, answers, and helpful advice to offer. There may have even been a time where you were just unsure about what to do next. It may not happen to everyone, but it definitely happens to some…even me. I'm going to be as transparent with you as possible because I believe it is important to connect with you in a way where you feel like you know me. I want you to know me and my struggles so you can see how I allowed them to not set me back but catapult me forward.

There was a time in my life where I felt things couldn't get any worse and they just wouldn't get better. For about two months I experienced set back after set back that just drained me and caused a mental and spiritual blockage. My mind didn't think at the level I knew it could and my faith was just not at its peak. I had never felt so empty, lost, or confused like this in my life. I didn't have the desire to write, work, or do anything period. I felt stuck. My family and I were evicted from our apartment. They gave us 3 days to find a new place to live. We couldn't find a place in three days so we had to temporarily move in with a friend of the family until we found a place. I went back and forth between my dad's house and the family friend's house. I felt homeless even still. In my eyes I was homeless. The places we had to stay weren't what I was used to nor what I wanted but I knew I had no choice but to make it work. Even though both my dad and the family friend were welcoming and very accommodating, especially under short notice and abrupt intrusion, those places weren't home. Nothing was mine at either place, all I had were the items I brought with me.

You would think I had enough motivation to do something with my life but I didn't. My everyday routine was to sleep, eat, catch up on television shows, go to sleep, and repeat it again the next day. In spite of me not feeling good about myself or my situation, I still wrote encouraging messages on my Facebook status every single day. It almost felt as though I had two people living inside of me. One person was extremely depressed about her situation and the other one didn't allow her situation to affect her faith or ability to encourage someone else. So what I did was suppress the one with all the faith and encouraging things to say and let depressed Rae rise up and come out. Of course, the devil had a ball with that. I forgot who I was. Because no one was really aware of the inner battle or breakdown I was having no one could really help me. I'm not one to really talk about if I'm feeling down or upset about something. I prefer to keep it to myself and handle it in my own way. Besides, me talking to someone else would force me to listen to how they would deal with MY situation and I didn't really feel as though that solution would help me. No one even knew about our living situation either. Everything was under wraps because who wants to be looked at like they can't pay rent or can't keep their house? No one.

I felt like I was dying on the inside and no one knew. I kept everything to myself because if I let one thing out I had to let the whole thing out in order for them to truly understand. I was angry, annoyed, frustrated, sad, fed up, unhappy, and to top it all off my boyfriend at that time was acting up. What a combination right? Right! Everything that could have gone wrong did go wrong. I cried for what others thought to be no reason but the truth of the matter was…I didn't feel like me anymore. I kept going to church but when I got back to the house I felt empty all over again. I didn't pray as much as I used to and felt as if I no longer had the ability to pray. I needed a push that would evoke self-restoration. I needed to put all these feelings to the side and focus on allowing the Spirit of God to lead me. As long as I continued to allow my emotions dictate how I viewed myself and my situation, I was a sinking ship. You can't follow feelings and God.

Taking control of your feelings is the key to taking authority over situations. The answer to all of my problems was to change my way of thinking and seek God. Some say it's easier said than done and I agree. All it takes is you opening your mouth and confessing the Word of God over your life. You will feel much better when you do. I felt lost because I strayed away from the Father who said He would never leave or forsake me. I ignored Him. He didn't ignore me or my problems. I didn't feel good about myself because I allowed my circumstances to speak louder than my faith. When you feel things take a turn in your life remember the promises God made to you. Be mindful of the fact that every storm must come to an end but its end date is solely up to you. You have to decree and declare the word of God over your life. Don't die in the storm. God made a way for you long ago. You have to go for it and believe it! Don't miss your exit out the storm. God wanted to be my refuge at the very beginning of my situation but I was stuck in the funk. The minute I changed my way of thinking my mom got a call that our new place was ready for us to move in. Not only that, I let go of that no good guy in my life and then the one I unknowingly prayed for came in and exemplified the Son of God! God will work things out for you every time but we cannot get weary in well doing. I had to remind myself who I was and get back to preparing myself for the world to see the hand of God move in my life. You have to make the choice to live and not die! You have to make the choice to rise up and be bigger than every situation you face. Take your strength back. Take your joy back. Get ready to get your wings because you endured long enough. This is your season!

Isaiah 40:31 (KJV)

"But they that wait upon the Lord shall renew their strength; they shall mount up with wings as eagles; they shall run, and not be weary; and they shall walk, and not faint."

Psalms 91:1-7 (NLT)

"Those who live in the shelter of the Most High will find rest in the shadow of the Almighty. This I declare about the LORD: He alone is my refuge, my place of safety; he is my God, and I trust him. For he will rescue you from every trap and protect you from deadly disease. He will cover you with his feathers. He will shelter you with his wings. His faithful promises are your armor and protection. Do not be afraid of the terrors of the night, nor the arrow that flies in the day. Do not dread the disease that stalks in darkness, nor the disaster that strikes at midday. Though a thousand fall at your side, though ten thousand are dying around you, these evils will not touch you."

-Rae

STAY UP

In life, you sometimes encounter many experiences causing you to be down for maybe a minute. You go through things causing you to take your focus off of God and on the situation at hand. When this occurs you can instantly become an easy target for the devil. The minute you remove yourself from the presence of God the devil is on the move and ready to try and keep you in guilt, sin, or worried about the present circumstance. He then has an open door to play with your thoughts and try to get you to believe the things God told you "yes" to are now a "no" or tell you your dreams can no longer come true because of natural circumstances. You become susceptible to the enemy's attacks when you dwell in his territory. It's almost like breaking into someone else's house. If they catch you, they have the right to harm you because you are on their property.

Operating in the natural is like playing in the devil's playground. He wants you to think and believe your life is horrible or that you will never amount to anything. The devil wants that boy to get all of your attention so you won't have any room for God. The devil wants you to feel like all the goals you set for yourself are unattainable. That is who he is and how he operates. He is low and because he is low you must Stay Up. Keep your head in the sky and your focus on God. Maintain a prevailing mindset!

You must always dwell in the presence of the Lord because that's where you find peace and fullness of joy. Do not continue to allow your situation to dictate your way of thinking. As long as you allow your circumstances to define you they will always confine you and that's exactly what the devil wants. You have to become superior to all you were once susceptible to. You have to live from an "on top" perspective. It's so easy to become trapped in a low state of being but it is so easy to get out as well. You must pray every single day.

The most powerful weapon you have on you at all times is your mouth. Speak over your life each and every day. Do not permit any negative way of thinking or speaking to overcome you. You were created to live and STAY on top. The devil doesn't have access to anything above his head. He does not have the advantages you have. But YOU, own an all-access pass. You can't access it by staying in that low place. Speak life into your life and speak highly of yourself at all times because nothing can stop you're on top. There are no impossibilities for you. Do not get tricked into thinking you cannot be what you want to be or do what you want to do.

Philippians 4:13 (MSG)

"Whatever I have, wherever I am, I can make it through anything in the One who makes me who I am."

That scripture should be enough to make you go out and pick up your victory. It's already yours and just waiting for you to pick it up. You are equipped with everything you need. God gave you access to everything when Jesus died on the cross, all you have to do is go out and get it. The only work you really have to do is walk into every situation with an "on top" perspective. You have the keys to every door. A faith-based thinking gets you in every door. You have the option to accept the negative report and drown in it or send it back with faith knowing everything is going to work out in your favor. Ride the wave of faith. As a believer of God, you are NOT to go with the flow, you are to create it! I challenge you to Stay Up and live with an on top perspective every day. Nothing can stop you!

-Rae

DATING AND RELATIONSHIP 101

SOLID FOUNDATION=GOOD COMMUNICATION

Before establishing a relationship with anyone it is imperative you establish a strong and solid foundation with God first. Time spent with God should be intimate, serious, important, and done every single day. You have to learn how to communicate with the one who has your very best interest at heart on a daily basis.

If you are new to all of this and really don't know what to do, just start by talking to God in the morning after you wake up. If your household is anything like mine, you may need to utilize your time in the shower to talk to God so you can have a little privacy when doing it. I have made the bathroom my prayer closet on many occasions and the conversations we have, God and I, has definitely been life changing. It was in my bathroom where I heard the Lord tell me to write this book. We were in mid conversation and I heard Him. Notice I said, "We" were in mid conversation, when in communication with God allow Him to speak to YOU. Prayer should not be a monologue but a dialogue between both you and God. What God has to say to us is much greater than what we have to say to Him. You will be surprised by the amount of times you feel the presence of God in the bathroom.

When your worship is for real, it doesn't matter where you are or when you feel it, you just go forth in it. When you are desperate you get what you need anywhere you can. Talks with God in the morning before you start your day should always make you feel good and refreshed. Those talks will cause things to shift in your life for the better.

During this time, you are learning to trust God to have His way in your life. You are learning to change whatever needs to be changed. You are yielding yourself to God as a willing vessel and allowing Him to use you in any way He can. Because our ways don't always work out, it is wise to allow God to have His way at all times. His plans never fail. A desire to please God is the best one to have. When we honor God, we allow ourselves to be honored by Him through His grace. He's waiting on us.

Deuteronomy 28:1 (NIV)

"If you fully obey the word of the Lord your God and carefully follow all His commands I give you today, the Lord your God will set you high above all the nations on Earth."

In order to be successful in every area of your life you have to live right and do right. My Grammie told me all the time, "When you know better, you do better." As we receive better, it is important that we apply it to our lives so we can get better results.

Proverbs 10:17 (NIV)

"Whoever heeds discipline shows the way to life, but whoever ignores correction leads others astray."

Pray without ceasing and worship God every time something good comes to mind.

- Rae

GET YOUR MIND RIGHT

With a change of direction comes a change of mind and a new plan of action. Every day is a new opportunity for you to do something different. When you change the level of your thinking you will change the level of your living.

It is never too late to turn over a new leaf. No matter what you have been faced with or facing, the present time is the best time to start fresh. Many people make the mistake in believing they have to wait until the new year to start fresh, but why put a delay on better? A great way to start is by writing out everything you need in order to be where you want to be in life. If going back to school is your heart's desire, then search the school/s of your choice and read their entry requirements so you will know what you need to do to start. If you want a car, look up some cars and find out how much you will have to save in order to attain the vehicle you want. If you don't have a job, see who is hiring and claim that job as yours every single day you wake up. Everything starts with a plan of action. You cannot keep skimming through life without a plan of action.

My Grammie used to say all the time "If better is possible, good is not enough". You must be hungry and thirsty for more and better for yourself. In life you have people who are hungry, content, and full. Stay hungry for greater and go get it. Do not starve yourself of success. Wanting better for yourself is a taste only YOU can acquire. Hungry people eat! Individuals who are content only worry about what is in front of them. Content people live for the moment and worry about tomorrow when it rolls around. The individuals who are full think they have enough and there is nothing else to do. The thing is, there is always more to have, learn, and obtain! Your work is never finished. You may think you're full but in all actuality you're just limiting yourself and God because there is more to do and more to acquire.

You have too much to offer this world for you to be sitting around bored every day. An idle mind is a playground for the devil.

Proverbs 16:27 (NIV)

"A scoundrel plots evil, and on their lips it is like scorching fire."

Do not give the devil room to play with your thoughts and get you doing things you shouldn't be.

It is time for you to get your life in order. The man God has for you does not want to find you all a mess. We have to be in right standing with God and have our lives on the right track. I challenge you to end all excuses today. Turn your situation around and get a move on. You cannot be stopped! There is greatness inside of you that the world is waiting to see and it requires you leaving your bedroom and putting your gifts to work. Make your family proud to have you in the family. Go walk in your destiny.

Romans 8:37 (NLT)

"No, despite all these things overwhelming victory is ours through Christ, who loved us."

1 John 4:4 (NLT)

"But you belong to God, my dear children. You have already won a victory over those people, because the spirit who lives in you is greater than the spirit who lives in the world."

-Rae

MISSION COMPLETE

Colossians 2:10 (NLT)

"So you are complete through your union with Christ, who is the head over every ruler and authority."

We often look to be fulfilled and completed by others rather than realizing we were made complete in Christ. It is easier for us to think of ourselves as being incomplete and needing someone to be the missing piece to our puzzle rather than taking the time out to tap into everything we already possess. We would rather settle to believe we need someone to complete us than to try to see what we don't feel, complete.

It is imperative you recognize you are complete. You must also find happiness within your complete self and about yourself before you try to find it in anyone else. Relationships only work when the two individuals are capable of identifying flaws within themselves before they identify flaws in each other. You can't help someone else be complete if you haven't realized you are already complete through Jesus Christ. You won't allow someone else to love what you do not love. That is why it is important for you to love yourself and every part of you. If you don't love your body how can someone else love it? You will always redirect their love from that area because you don't love that area yourself. Most relationships fall to shambles because one person is in total denial of who they are or one doesn't even know who they are. You cannot show a person how to love you if you don't even love you.

Stop trying to jump into relationships with the hopes of finding the missing piece to your puzzle. You are the missing piece to your puzzle! Once you realize you have everything you need to make it and get through life with ease you will stop searching for someone else to make things easy for you. You are the cause of your life being hard due to you putting your faith in relationships to make you whole rather than allowing God to fill the voids in your life. If you allow man to build you up instead of God, be prepared for man to take all their bricks when you upset him. God will build you up, make you strong, and not take a thing away when you walk away from Him. Unbeknownst to you, your cup is running over but you are so blinded by everything natural. A good relationship starts with a good YOU! Ask God to help you see what He sees and help you feel everything you are. Thank God for vision like His. People can only meet you as deep as you've met yourself. It's time for you to dig deep and meet who you really are and who you were created to be. You have had enough relationships built in shallow water, it's time for you to swim in the deep end with someone. Take the time out to evaluate you and learn about yourself.

Being complete is not the result of being in a relationship with man, it's the result of being in relationship with Christ. People are looking to others to make up for their deficiencies. How do you know you are complete? You know when you are secure and satisfied in relationship with God. If you are single and dissatisfied, then it is a clear indication you are not complete in God. To be complete is to be whole, nothing missing and nothing broken. When one cannot be happy in God alone one is not prepared for relationship with anyone else. You do not determine when you are ready, God does. As a reward of making God your focus, He will cause the right one to put their focus on you. Hallelujah! Thank you Lord for your Word!

-*Rae*

DON'T BELIEVE THE HYPE

Society and social media do an awesome job of making youth feel rushed to get into relationships. It seems as though it's the only thing that matters today when of course, it isn't. I believe it is difficult to not feel like you are behind or missing out on something when every time you log on to social media you see "relationship goals" plastered everywhere that are not even ideal for the younger generation. In spite of everything society says, it is okay to be single and on hold until you have reached all your personal goals. It's okay to wait for a God-sent individual to find you whole and ready. Do not make the mistake of allowing social media dictate when the time is right for you to date or be in a relationship.

The generation of today also makes the mistake of caring so much about outer appearance that they have lost focus of what really makes one likable. It seems as though no one cares about having a good attitude, being respectful, manners, or anything that should count for that matter. As women of God, there has to be a distinction between us and women of the world. We are supposed to be the example for the women who are not saved. We should be looked up to because of how we carry ourselves differently from the rest of the world. We have the Glory of God all over us but yet it is not recognized because we have diluted ourselves just to blend in with everyone else. Real men are still seeking women of virtue. Real men are not just interested in what is appealing to the eye but also what one has to offer besides being cute. There is nothing wrong with a man wanting a woman because she is beautiful, but looks should not be the only thing she can bring to the table.

Proverbs 31:30 (NLT)

"Charm is deceptive, and beauty does not last; but a woman who fears the LORD will be greatly praised."

Society has confused us when it comes to when we should be in a relationship, when we should be married, and all the way to what a beautiful woman looks like. Do not permit anyone to make you doubt your progress in this world nor your beauty. You are smart, gifted, and because you were created in the image of God you are beautiful. Recognize your worth and walk in confidence knowing you are not behind in life, everyone else is just moving way too fast. When you are driving a car too fast you are bound to have a collision at some point. Own what you have and rock your confidence. If you don't receive your confidence from people get it from the Word of God.

Ephesians 2:10 (NLT)

"For we are God's masterpiece. He has created us anew, in Christ Jesus, so we can do the good things he planned for us long ago."

-Rae

PRAY AND WAIT

Psalms 37:4 (KJV)

"Delight thyself also in the Lord; and he shall give thee the desires of thine heart."

Matthew 21:22 (KJV)

"And all things, whatsoever ye shall ask in prayer, believing, ye shall receive."

Nothing is too hard for God. As long as what we want is in alignment with His word nothing is off limits. It's okay to pray to God about the kind of man you want to find you. What you can do is make a list of all the characteristics, features, traits, and attributes you want this man to have and claim it as yours every day. There is nothing wrong with knowing what you want. While you are delighting yourself in the Lord and allowing Him to steer you in the right direction you can be sure God will give you exactly what your heart desires. It is in the word!

While waiting, focus on getting yourself together so there will be no bumps in the road when the man you prayed for finds you. You should want to be ready and equipped with all things necessary to work the relationship. Keep yourself busy while in waiting. Do not get yourself distracted by the side attractions that may look good but mean you no good. Stay in constant communication with God so you can hear every word He has to say.

There are times where you may feel weak and tempted to get side tracked by other things but pray for strength to resist the devil so he will flee. The power of life and death are in the words we speak. By speaking things into existence we have the power to control our lives. For example, whenever we feel tempted to do something we know is wrong, by simply speaking and believing "I will resist temptation and the devil will flee", the devil is going to back off. The devil will definitely try to trick you into thinking there is a void in your life needing to be filled by a man. You should immediately shut down all those thoughts and know you have been made complete in Christ Jesus. Patience is a virtue every strong woman needs to have. By the time you get to the finish line you will be glad you waited because the man you really want will be wrapped up in all your desires and created especially for you. Don't give in too early because you just might lose out on what you always wanted. Beware of distractions and the devil.

- *Rae*

IDENTIFYING THE CHOSEN ONE

Everyone is not for you. This includes people you meet, date, and possibly a few friends. On this journey through life, you will have random people come in your life whom you think you have to be open to because you believe they've been sent by God, but most times they haven't. They're usually sent by the devil just to throw you off course. Watch out, your flesh may get weak for them, but do not give in because the one God has for you is on the way!

Every time we fall short and off track, we're usually just 7 feet away from what God has for us. I don't mean a literal 7 feet, but a spiritual 7-foot distance. In other words, we are closer than we think and only set closer when we are paying attention to God and not our fleshly desires. I'm sure you've heard the saying, "follow your heart", but quite often, following your heart can lead you right into a heartbreak. I have lost count of how many times I've "followed my heart" and landed myself in a bush full of pain and regret. The best thing to do is to follow the voice of God and trust His plan. Stay so connected to God you do not even want to make a move without Him giving you His approval. Following your heart sounds good and may even feel good in the beginning but trust me, following God is way better.

The company you keep is something of which you need to continuously keep in mind. Do not allow people to come and tempt you to sin and give in to your flesh. If a guy wants to "talk" to you and get to know you on a more personal level do not let him come to your house. You should meet him outside of your house, like at a restaurant or a plan a fun outing. Your house should not be a date night option. You shouldn't want to put yourself in a situation that has the potential to take you off your spiritual journey. You do not want to land yourself into something you wish you would have never gotten yourself into. If the guy does come to your house, make sure there are people around who won't allow things to go left and downhill. When I say go left, I mean take you off the course God has put you on and into a trap the devil has been waiting to catch you in. Invite the guy over only when all of your friends are there or when your family is having a game night or get-together. When no one is home and the two of you are alone, it is easy for an atmosphere of sin to be set and things which should not happen are now prone to happen.

Discontinue allowing those "can I come see you" or "come see me" guys in your life. They usually only want one thing and come with a host of lies and excuses as to why they cannot be serious with you. Your focus should be on the person who wants to take you "out", not the one who wants to stay "in". The difference between a boy and a man is one only wants to Netflix and chill while having lustful desires to lure you into ungodly activities and a man has pure intentions to take you out on real dates and prove to you why you should allow him to be more than just a friend without any strings attached. A boy doesn't think he has anything to prove to you. A boy with hidden agendas believes he should just have everything you have to offer all to himself based off of his good looks alone. A man knows there is work to be done to get you as the leading lady in his life. A man knows and realizes you do not have time for games and doesn't want to fumble your heart. The man who is sent from God will get to know you clothes on, before anything else. When you are weak and vulnerable he will never cross the line with you because he doesn't ever want to offend you or cause you to feel uncomfortable around him. Your job is to always stand your ground and not give into your flesh. A real man will only go as far as you let him and if you have already notified him of your personal ground rules and he respects your wishes, don't switch it up just because he agrees to them. You must remember you are a woman of God who won't allow a small respectable moment cause you to change your mind about saving yourself until marriage. You deserve respect and just because a man shows you respect doesn't mean you owe him your treasure.

Always keep in mind you are worth waiting for. You have to get used to people treating you with respect no matter who didn't in the past. A man showing you and giving you respect does not deserve anything more than a thank you. Do not over compensate. If it doesn't work don't force it. If you have to force it then it isn't meant for you. The one chosen by God for you will never need you to beg them to stay in your life. You will not have to force a God-sent man. Never lose sight of what you want in a man or in a relationship.

Proverbs 18:22 (NIV)

"He who finds a wife finds what is good and receives favor from the LORD."

Your job is to wait on God to send you the man of your dreams. You have no business looking for a man to love you and treat you right. A man finds a wife, not the other way around. When the time is right all of these things will fall into place in the way it should.

- Rae

CHECK YOURSELF

We often look for the perfect person for ourselves but who are we perfect for? We want the people who are interested in dating us to have all the right qualities, say all the right things, and do all the right stuff but can we reciprocate the same characteristics? No one is perfect and because of it, no relationship will be perfect. There will be problems which come up here and there and maybe even a few disagreements but the way you decide to handle them and work through them will be the helpful tool in deciding who is the best candidate for you.

I used to think if there were disagreements and a lot of misunderstandings in the relationship then the person was not my intended mate. In some cases, it can be proven true but not in all of them. I was always the one ready to leave when things got rough because I never wanted to feel like I was settling for less than the best. Growing up, I saw how unhappy my parents were together so I always used them as a reference tool whenever I decided to let go of a relationship. I asked myself all the time, "Does this look like Bob and Dev's situation?" I had a firsthand glance at what settling for someone for reasons other than love looked like. I promised myself I would never make the same mistake.

You have to understand this, every single relationship is going to have some problems. There is not a single person in this world you will be able to get into a relationship with and not have a few disagreements with here and there. If you realize it now, then the way you deal with people and how you relate with the person you are in a relationship with will change for the better. You have to stop expecting things to be perfect. That is the quickest way to run a good person away. You make them believe their efforts aren't enough and unknowingly make them feel inadequate for you. In the end, you cause them to no longer have a desire to be with you or maybe even love you in a way you would want them to love you.

I had this conversation with my dad and he asked me, "Do you love God?" Of course I said yes. He said, "Have you done things you know He doesn't like for you to do?" I replied, "yes." "Does He still love you?" he asked. "Yes of course He does!" I answered. "Then why can't you show a little grace when someone hurts you? Why can't you still love the person who made a mistake?" my dad questioned. I had to think about it for a little while. My dad has always been my go to for relationship advice and this time he had me in deep thought. Unbeknownst to me I was doing the very thing to people I would never want God to do to me. We want God to love us in spite of the fact we sin daily. A person messes up with us one time and we are often ready to crucify them and turn our backs on them without question. It isn't fair. You have to operate with others the way God operates with you. Everyone makes mistakes but just like God, we have to give one another a chance to redeem ourselves. If you can talk with the person about the mistakes you've made, recognize them, and not experience the same ones over and over then you all are on the right track. Don't allow anyone to run over you and make up excuses as to why they can't be what you need them to be. That isn't love. Love is when both parties can acknowledge their wrong and work towards not making the same mistake again.

Try not to run away so quickly so you can see the improvements and adjustments the people you love make for you. Give people a chance to grow and show you they can do better and be better for you. The right one will want to be better for you because he won't want to give you any reason to make you feel like he isn't a match for you. The right one will be right and do right by you! You have to learn how to give what you'd want to receive whether it be love, forgiveness, loyalty, or honesty. If you cannot give it then your hand should not be open for it because it cannot be given by you. You must give to receive.

Matthew 6:14-15 (MSG)

"In prayer there is a connection between what God does and what you do. You can't get forgiveness from God, for instance, without also forgiving others. If you refuse to do your part, you cut yourself off from God's part."

Do not expect what you yourself cannot offer.

-Rae

BE NOT DECEIVED

There are many signs shown to us that indicate "deceit ahead" and we should in fact be mindful of these signs. The first major sign is when a guy says he is not looking for a relationship, but clearly wants more than just a regular friendship. This usually means he just wants relations with no strings attached and no commitment. If a man really wants to be with you, he won't allow anything to hold him back or get in his way. The same one not looking for a relationship wants the benefits given as if he is in a relationship. They want to come over, kiss, cuddle, talk late at night, and possibly a little more. See, when you give in you are allowing him to have access to everything for which he is unqualified. Why would he want to get in a relationship with you after you let him in without clearance? You gave away all of your valuables without the man having to pay a price. While he is getting everything he wants with no strings attached, you're stuck with feelings and emotions you don't know what to do with because he doesn't want to be your man. He only wants you when it is convenient for him. He can't reciprocate all your feelings because he told you from jump he wasn't ready for strings to be attached and you let him in anyway. You can't be mad when the feelings aren't mutual because you screwed yourself over. He was straightforward while you were clouded by your desire right? You wanted his mind to curve just a little bit so you gave him all of you thinking it would change his mind but it didn't. The only thing it changed was how he looked at you and how you felt about yourself.

Guys sometimes want a lot without giving anything substantial or concrete in return. Why? Well, we as women have allowed guys to think it is okay to take without them being worthy. We've made these men comfortable in thinking it is okay to take and not give. It is completely on us as women. We set the standards for ourselves. If we set our assets at the bottom shelf it wouldn't make sense for guys to reach for whatever is at the top. If we make them work their way to the top they will see the best things in life come with a price. A price must be paid to acquire all you have to offer a man and that price is a commitment through marriage. As a woman, you should be a package deal and a man should not be able to do just one thing to gain access to everything. You would be cheating yourself if you ever allowed this to occur. If a man wants all of you he has to go through the levels it takes to obtain all of you. If he wants your love he has to give you a commitment plus loyalty. If he wants your body, then he has to give you a marriage and not just a ring with unfulfilled promises attached. If he wants your attention, he has to show you effort and give you his time. If he wants you to trust him he has to prove to you he is trustworthy and never give you a reason to believe he isn't.

Good things never come easy or fast. Stop making men think they don't have to work for anything. Relationships should be an even trade where both individuals give 100% no matter what. You can't give $50 and expect $100 in change. It doesn't work like that. Chivalry is not dead and women of class, virtue, integrity, and respect have not gone extinct. You are a Queen and must be treated as such and should definitely act accordingly. Respect yourself enough not to give everyone the opportunity to say they have had you. Save yourself for the one who marries you because he has shown himself to be worthy. You must realize everyone does not deserve you. If you are one who has already given yourself to someone or maybe even a few people you are not disqualified from being a Queen or from making the next man wait. A guy may try to trick you by making you think you aren't worth waiting for because you aren't a virgin but that's a lie. The most important thing is you being on the right track now and learning from your past mistakes. God can make any old thing new and restore everything you once lost to someone who did not deserve it. The blood has washed away all of your sins but you have to make a conscious decision to follow God and His word. You can be made new today by committing to live a life of celibacy until you are married. You are worth the wait and then some. You may be copper, silver, or bronze today but God can make you platinum tomorrow if you just commit to Him from here on out. Don't give another man access to what they haven't worked for. You may think it is hard right now but your reward will be great and will exceed your expectations. God has someone for you who will appreciate, love, cherish, protect, and be faithful to you. You just have to wait on Him! Don't fall into the traps Satan will set up for you. Stay close to God and far from sin. He will see you through.

- Rae

"IN ALL THY GETTINGS…"

One of the biggest problems we as women have is trying to force or invoke a change in someone who is completely comfortable with themselves and how they go about doing things. You cannot make someone change when they do not see anything wrong with themselves. You do not have the power to change the mind of someone else. The person must be willing and have a desire to want to change on their own.

You can be all a person needs and everything they need you to be, but if the person is not ready to receive and appreciate you then you have to back off. Never try to force a man or anyone else to see the greatness you possess. They have to want to open their eyes and accept what they have in front of them.

I went through this lesson a few times. I've gone through this with so many different people on so many different occasions. I had to do a self-evaluation check. I had to realize what I was doing wrong and what I needed to stop doing. One of those things being me explaining myself in such an elaborate way that's full of details. I thought doing that made me easier to understand, but the person on the other side always found it to be too much to grasp. With the help of my dad and the Holy Spirit I came to the conclusion it was not that my concept was too difficult to understand, but just that the other person didn't have a desire to understand me. In order for you to get a new understanding you must first be open to it.

While in a relationship you should always be open to attempting to get an understanding with your partner and allowing yourself to view things from their perspective. If the person you are with doesn't want to understand you then they are not ready to be in a relationship.

Proverbs 4:7 (NIV)

"The beginning of wisdom is this: Get wisdom. Though it cost all you have, get understanding."

Proverbs 4:7 (NLT)

"Getting wisdom is the wisest thing you can do! And whatever else you do, develop good judgement."

A wise man always wants to be clear and eliminate all confusion. If the person you are with doesn't mind leaving you confused, then you need to leave them right where they are. A man shouldn't want his woman to feel like she is misunderstood or like she isn't being heard. A man should make sure his woman knows he is listening to everything she has to say and taking everything into consideration. Stop allowing the devil to write your story. If you are constantly confused, then stop giving the devil the pen and give it to God.

1 Corinthians 14:33 (KJV)
"For God is not the author of confusion, but of peace, as in all churches of the saints."

Release your pen from the devil and turn it over to God. Release your heart from the one who doesn't want to hear it and wait for God to send you someone who wants to hear and understand everything you have to say. Recognize the signs early so you won't feel trapped with feelings and emotions later on down the line. You do not have to let the paint dry to find out what color it is.

-Rae

FOLLOW SUIT

There are a plethora of things I've learned about myself during the single stages of my life. Many of which having to do with relationships. I didn't just learn what my true desire was in a relationship, but also what I didn't want or need as well. Relationships are serious and should always be regarded as such. Giving your heart to someone without limitations, guards, or restrictions is serious, but not everyone realizes it. It is extremely important for you to have this wisdom so whoever you meet can either follow suit or get the boot.

At one point in time I thought I understood this information enough to put it to the test. The moment I was ready to begin the process of dating things took a turn for me. I was thrown mixed signals by the guy I was pursuing at the time and it landed me flat on my butt with all kinds of misunderstanding. He didn't know what he wanted and from that I learned a mixed signal from someone else can be a very clear and obvious sign for you. Your job is to take it and go. We sometimes have a tendency to want to ponder on things too long and to the point where we no longer want to get out the jam but more so use our confusion as a conversation starter for the potential suiter. When you know exactly where you want to be and want out of a relationship it won't be hard to toss out the pens which don't write or shall I say, the guys who aren't working right for you. You should want someone who is going to add to the unfinished lines you have on your page of life. One who can help things make sense, not someone who will ruin what you have and cause you to have to start all over.

You should want consistency. It is one of the key ingredients to a successful relationship. If one is consistently inconsistent why would you have a desire to make them a constant in your life? Knowing yourself includes knowing your limits; how much you can tolerate from a person and how much you can't. If you have already reached your limits during the time you guys are just supposed to be getting to know one another, you can only imagine how many occasions you will reach your limits while in a relationship with this person. It is imperative you recognize the signs of "destruction ahead" at their first appearance so all ties can be severed before you all get too serious. Don't get linked to someone longer than you should be.

Dating is the process before getting into a relationship and is also a time for you two to learn one another. While dating, you all aren't bound by any laws, vows, or long term commitments. Therefore, if you don't agree or like something he does you can leave with no strings attached and really no explanation needed. It is okay to keep your options open if you all aren't official or exclusive. Dating one person is fine but don't be so wrapped up in it you go crazy over someone who doesn't belong to you. In my opinion, it is the quickest way to get in your feelings. Why you may ask…Well, you tend to forget he is not obligated to text you back immediately, free to not call you every night, and free to come around when he feels like it and not every time you want him to. You all are not in a relationship so therefore you all are not obligated to meet each other's needs ALL the time.

It's important you set the tone in the beginning so no boundaries are crossed. You determine what is acceptable and what will and will not be tolerated. If you have no desire to chill and watch movies at each other's houses, then you have to make it known when the suggestion is brought up. You don't march to the beat of a man's drum who is not your husband, you create the beat until you have a marriage. Let's not get this confused for not allowing the man to be the man in a relationship. You allow him to be the man who respects you and your wishes. That's it, that's all. Don't allow these guys to get too comfortable too soon. When you make him comfortable too early he then gets in the mindset of thinking he already has you when in reality, he doesn't.

There is still work to be done. You are a gift which can't be unwrapped twice. Therefore, you are not easily attainable. There is always more to do. Stand firm in your beliefs and make everyone else adjust to you.

-Rae

HEAVEN SENT V.S. WE PICKED

Many times we make the mistake of proclaiming a rocky relationship to be a blessing in disguise or one which could help mold us or make us better later. In most cases it is true. Our mishaps and mistakes help us learn and make ourselves better for the next person but it doesn't mean God sent those people to hurt us or break our hearts. This is not how God operates. He is loving, sweet, and caring. God doesn't need to make bad things happen to you in order to teach you a lesson. Those lessons usually get taught due to you straying away from God and His will for your life. We get ourselves caught up in things we should have never been in from the very beginning. Only good comes from God. Leave the wickedness to Satan or your own poor judgment of a person.

James 1:17 (KJV)

"Every good gift and every perfect gift is from above, and cometh down from the Father of the lights, with whom is no variableness, neither shadow of turning."

It's time to start recognizing the demons in our lives for who they are and act accordingly. People talk about blessings in disguise all the time but to be honest, most blessings are recognizable. When a person has truly been sent from God it will not be hard to tell because they will operate like their creator/sender. They will be kind, sweet, and nice like the one who sent them. A God sent individual understands their assignment to be good to you and does it without you having to ask. When this person comes along you may be taken back by all the sweet gestures, compliments, and their desire to see you happy because you came across a few imposters in the past. But the thing you must know is with a God-sent, things like this are just in their nature. It doesn't stop after getting to know them or 5 months later. It's a continued thing because it is just what they do. Those who were not sent by God will be just like Satan, a liar and deceiver too. The real deal will be the same today and tomorrow as he was yesterday and the day before. People who are sent from God do not change up like the seasons nor do they require you to walk on eggshells with them. They really don't require much of you at all other than you being yourself at all times. Those Heaven sent individuals are not looking to count favors or exchange anything with you for what they give you but yet you still question everything they do and want to know why they're doing it because it's nothing like you are used to. You give them a hard time because before them, someone else who did a few similar things had an ulterior motive and you are suspicious. However, this person is genuine, no ulterior sinister motives. Elevation causes you to be uncomfortable because you are now in a new place. You've been treated like bottom-shelf material for so long you forgot how it feels to be the one someone is reaching up for. You are so used to guys coming at you sideways that when one is straightforward you think you are secretly under attack. When God raises you up, there will be no strings attached to pull you back down. You won't owe anyone anything for your elevation. You got used to the world pulling you and leaving you with nothing to show for it in the end. Elevation requires you to be separated from all which you were accustomed. Once a King has found his Queen she realizes everyone else had to have only thought of her as a peasant based on how they treated her. You may think you are undeserving, but a Heaven sent man believes you deserve it all and so much more. He does his best to show you and give it to you.

These types of individuals don't come when we want them but once we get to know them, we begin to wish they had found us just a little bit sooner. Everything happens unexpectedly but yet at the right time. Again, just like the sender, they are always there when you need them most. You see the God in them.

Stop wasting your time waiting for the silver coin to turn gold and focus on God to send you platinum. Never stop believing in God to give you your heart's desires. Your time is coming. Keep preparing yourself to be great. Stop picking them and let God send them!

If your God-sent man is in your life already and this chapter confirmed it for you, let him be great to you! I know it's hard, but know that God doesn't place anyone in your life to hurt you. Continue to pray the Lord directs your path and watch God continue to blow your mind by proving to you he is the one. He can only be what you allow him to be.

-Rae

TAKING BACK CONTROL

The biggest lesson I learned was to never put your significant other on a higher pedestal than God. You may be thinking to yourself, "Well how can you do that Rae?" It's so easy to do and happens so fast we don't catch it until the relationship is in shambles. Think about it, when in a relationship the first person we communicate with after we wake up isn't God it's our boyfriend. We haven't prayed or thanked God for another day but yet we texted "Bae". God should come first then "Bae". As long as God comes first in your life and in your relationship everything else will follow.

I made this very mistake and because of it, I experienced the worst heartbreak of my life. God didn't hurt me, I hurt myself when I excluded God from my relationship. If you aren't listening to God, He isn't going to speak. In this particular relationship, I should have been listening because I know God would have told me this person wasn't for me out the gate. But, at that time God was not my primary focus which made me think I lost Him and then caused me to lose my true identity.

It was my senior year in high school and I found myself to be so deeply in love with this person, I began to lose myself in him. He was musically-inclined, talented, sweet when he desired to be, charismatic, stylish, and got me whatever I wanted just to say the least. We came across too many issues to be a match made in Heaven but I can say when we were good we were great. There wasn't an in between with us. Nonetheless, this guy had my heart, emotions, and my mind. He had me completely captivated. Every time I thought I wanted out he had no problem directing me to the door but I always closed the door and locked myself back in. He didn't care about letting me go which is what I couldn't understand. Although he wasn't the best thing for me I didn't want to see myself without him. I lost myself so much I became his puppet. Every time he did something wrong my entire mood would change for the worse and wouldn't go back until he fixed it or changed it. No man should have that kind of control over you. It's unhealthy. I allowed him to have more power and more influence over my life than God had. He had the remote to my happiness and flipped it whenever he felt like it.

I eventually came to a point where I had to choose to stay or go. I knew I should have left when he cheated multiple times, wasn't being supportive, verbally abusive, or at the moment I realized he didn't respect me but I didn't. I thought things would get better but in cases like mine you don't wait for things to improve, you have to leave at the first sign that indicates the person was not sent from God. Don't allow anyone to trample over your feelings. You are better than what any man says or thinks about you. At that point, you are ultimately hurting yourself because you can leave that person who keeps you bound.

It took me a year and 3 months to be tired of not feeling good enough, pretty enough, or acceptable for him so I ended the relationship. It was one of the hardest things I had to do because I just wanted him to change for me, or maybe just fight for me to be in his life but he didn't. He asked me was I sure about the decision I made and went on with his life like he never cared about me. That hurt me so bad I sunk myself into a depression. I lived in my pitch black room with dark blankets nailed to the windows preventing all sunlight from seeping through. I didn't eat and cried myself to sleep every night for a week. I had become weak and regretful for doing what was best for me. How does that even happen? I could have just stayed and had him in my life and been semi-happy. That sounded like a better idea but I knew deep down I did the best thing.

A week later my friend invited me to church and for the first time in a long time, I felt something other than pain and misery. I felt relief. At that church, I experienced my first breakthrough. I made a conscious decision to receive deliverance from everything and everyone who kept me in emotional bondage. I cried so much that night because I finally got the relief I longed for and what I needed to overcome depression. I was glad my friends forced me to go to church that day. I was happy my mom prayed for me and for my situation. During my state of depression, I prayed too. I didn't want to feel like I did but I knew I had to do something. I allowed the enemy to attack my thoughts and trick me into thinking that I wouldn't find anyone better.

If only you trust God and seek his face during your lowest moments, they will turn out to be your best moments. When I left that person, it did not feel good, but it was the best decision I could have ever made. Leaving that toxic relationship forced me to reconnect with God. We should have never lost connection in the first place. God gave me the courage to leave that hurt person who constantly hurt me. Hurt people can only hurt other people. Even if you are not the cause of their pain. Until they heal they can only hurt others to cover up for their hurting selves. God turned my tears of sorrow into tears of joy. I found the joy that was lost inside of me. I was able to get back into my word, prayer life, and I even started a daily devotion routine. I recognized myself again and knew I was more than enough. I felt beautiful again.

Someone out there is looking for you. If you are dealing with a toxic situation such as this one just begin to speak life over yourself. Do not fall into the devil's trap of making you believe nothing good will come to you. If you do not leave what's bad for you how will you know what is good? How can you experience good? God wants the best for our lives and it is up to us to trust Him to give it to us. This situation showed me who I should have put my trust in, from the beginning. Man will fail you daily but God never fails to deliver. Just when you thought God left you because you left Him, He shows up to remind you that He will never leave or forsake you.

Romans 8:28 (KJV)

"And we know that all things work together for good to them that love God, to them who are the called according to His purpose."

This toxic relationship ended up working for my good. It felt shaky in the beginning but regardless of what anyone else thought about me, I STILL came out on top. God is always ready to take us back and pick us up when we fall. That is a God worth putting first. You have to fully commit to God before you try committing to someone else. God is consistent when we aren't so why can't you commit? God honors us when we don't honor Him so why can't you commit? His loyalty to us can never be questioned. God always proves to us He is more deserving than the people we choose to be in our lives. Once we put God first and consult with Him before making a decision our lives would be less hectic.

Isaiah 40:31 (KJV)

"But they that wait upon the Lord shall renew their strength; they shall mount up with wings as eagles; they shall run, and not be weary, and they shall walk, and not faint."

A relationship with God is the best one to have.

-Rae

REPOSITION YOURSELF

It takes repositioning in order to see someone's true colors or true intentions. Just because you are close to someone doesn't mean you know everything there is to know about them nor does it mean you have seen all of the sides of this particular person. We tend to believe we have seen it all or can identify every single thing about a person by simply standing in one spot and it is untrue. It takes repositioning in order to get a better view and understanding of people. We have to constantly move around, press buttons, and ask questions and sometimes even that doesn't work. The best thing you can do is step back and just watch how things playout without you in the picture. You will never see all there is to see standing right upon the picture. You only catch a glimpse and small portion, mostly just the parts that interest you. We get so focused on bits and pieces we think there is nothing more to see. We blind ourselves with the false assumption of there is nothing more we need to pay attention to.

Sometimes you must take a few steps back to view an individual as they are and not as the person they have the potential to become. Your view may be closer than others, but that is a clear indication of you missing the reason why everyone else is standing so far away. You won't give yourself enough space to see what others may be warning you about. You haven't gotten to know this person from every angle, view, or position. Take the time out to reposition yourself and understand why people call them a liar, cheater, back stabber, manipulator, selfish, disloyal, abuser, or crowd pleaser. You could learn from other people but you choose to do the damage to yourself. You can't go off everything everyone says about a person, but at least be mindful of *what* they say and just take a step back far enough where you aren't the one hurt in the end. Don't be stuck wishing you listened to everyone else. In the end, be grateful you got the understanding for yourself.

Today I want you to take the time out to reposition yourself so you can see everything clearly. The further the better and once you've gotten your understanding then you can proceed. You'd be surprise at what you find out about the people closest to you.

-*Rae*

CTRL + ALT + DELETE

When God removes someone out of your life and closes the door on that particular chapter the best thing we can do is lock the door and throw away the key. Do not try and go after a person God wants to protect you from. God is definitely in the business of revealing individuals to us who have not been sent by Him, but He isn't the only one who can remove them. We have that responsibility as well. Once God does His part we have to make sure we do ours in keeping ourselves safe from emotional hurt and keeping closed doors locked. When God reveals to us who a person really is we should not second guess it because His opinion is always a fact! You have to trust God, believe, and know He has not forgotten about you. Your time is coming!

We often make the mistake of thinking we are over an ex until we see them with someone else and all those emotions, feelings, and memories start running back to us. We may even start to feel like we want to retract and try again with the individual. You begin comparing yourself to your ex's current mate and get yourself all rallied up and upset. I'm here to tell you to not be the person to go after an individual who you know is not a good fit for you. The only reason it starts happening is because of you being in a temporary emotional state. Use wisdom and remember the hurt and pain the person caused you and begin to thank God you dodged a bullet! Instead of being mad at the new girl he is with, praise God simply because it's not you and pray for her strength to deal with the things to come which she hasn't experienced yet. Everyone does not deserve to be in your life, so rejoice in the fact you got away before it was too late.

Everyone you encounter is not on your team. People will switch up in a minute and not think twice about it. The same person who smiled in your face and complimented your relationship can turn around and be your ex's new girlfriend. This is why constant communication with God is vital because it will enable and enhance your discerning spirit so you can properly recognize those who have pure intentions and those who don't. You can't be mad, bitter, or salty with these kind of individuals because it is what they have come to do. Their role is to cause discord but if you know you got out the jam, why be upset about who is next in line to go through the same hell and hot water you went through? Do not worry about the trash you throw out, let waste management do its job. Wait on the best for it is yet to come your way. Wait for the one God has promised you. You've read the story plenty of times and know the ending. Giving the book to someone else is the least you could do. You took the class, learned what you needed to know, now it's time to let someone else take it. You know a man knows when he had a good woman and lost her when he comes back asking for another chance to get it right. When you are no longer interested in the games and foolery, all he is left to do is move on which is what you should want anyway. Never let them see you sweat. You know what you were to him and he knows also. Every time he sees you he will remember.

-*Rae*

BETTER NOT BITTER

Over the years I've seen countless movies and real life situations where the wife/girlfriend gets dumped and she turns into this really bitter individual. It's sad because instead of trying to assess the issues and figure out what went wrong, the woman makes a conscious decision to go through life with the belief of every man is a dog. Every man isn't a dog. Every man doesn't cheat. It doesn't hurt to want a male companion in your life as your husband. I'm sure there have been times where you were alone at a party or celebration of some kind and just wished you had someone to share the moment with. It's okay if you have, as women we were not created to be alone forever. We were created to have male companionship. Due to us not following the order in which God set to do things, we often find ourselves like the bitter women on the movie screens; alone and mad.

God's order is not designed to fail. We fail because we do not operate in His order. We have to realize and understand where we go wrong in relationships. We know when things are taking a left turn and it is solely up to us to address it in order to protect our feelings, emotions, and most importantly the order of God. No matter what is going on our position must be made clear and concise so there is no room left for confusion on both ends of the relationship. It all goes back to making the person you are in relationship with or pursuing a relationship with aware of what you want and what is expected. Allow your demands and expectations to be recognized for the individual to adhere to them. They can either take it or leave it.

Women are emotional creatures. Physical interaction is not the bottom line for us. We think about how a man can stimulate our minds, how one can treat us, personalities, how he acts around his family, and how one thinks. When a guy breaks up with you it is so easy to become bitter, angry, and upset but you can't be. Why? Well, most times it is because of you not doing what you were supposed to do in the beginning to protect yourself which also includes abiding by God's set order. When you experience a break up, don't let him see you sweat. Instead, you should take the opportunity to work on yourself going forth. Remember, you're just a step closer to who you are meant to be with. Don't force anything and definitely don't burn your bridges because he could turn around, come back, and be all you ever wanted. It could just take you being more equipped, ready, mature, and open to receive him. Learn from your mistakes so you won't have to keep repeating the lesson. Don't dwell on negativity especially via social media. Perfect yourself and attract positivity only. Always set yourself up for success.

-Rae

MY PRAYER FOR YOU

I pray this book not only inspired you but uplifted and motivated you as well. As young women, we have to not only stick together, but work together also. I pray you received all of the information given to you with an open heart. I pray you ended the last chapter with a fresh focus, clean heart, and renewed spirit. I pray you know and believe you have been beautifully created inside and out and stand boldly on the fact no one can take your confidence or joy away from you. I pray you follow the lead of God and have a positive impact on everyone you encounter. I come against fear in your life to be different and pray you boldly take a stand for Christ and your beliefs. I come against the spirit of confusion and pray you have clarity of thought in every deliberation process. I pray you make wise decisions that will never cease to elevate you. In all you do, I pray an infinite amount of success over your life. I pray you begin every day and endeavor with Christ at the beginning, center, and end. I pray God gives you wisdom, guidance, peace, and strength to make it to the finish line. I pray you never forget to help the person behind you and help them know they are not alone. I pray you never forget where you've been and use your experiences to reach people right where they are. I pray the sincerity of my words reach, touch, and resonate with your heart. Thank you for gifting me this opportunity to pour into you all I have to give. May God keep, cover, and bless you always.

- Rae

ABOUT THE AUTHOR

Raelyn T. Purham is an advocate for young girls and believes with the right help, enough time, and proper guidance each girl can live a life without repeating the mistakes made by former generations. She believes generational curses can be broken through the sharing of life experiences, proper understanding of who God is, knowing how He operates, and identifying the purpose for which He created us. As the founder of Daughters of Destiny, a female Christian youth group, she works as a mentor while being the support to others she wish she had as a teenager. Raelyn understands that everyone has a story but not everyone has support. She is eager to change the lives of young ladies and introduce them to who God is while assisting them in identifying themselves through Christ. You can find out more about Raelyn T. Purham and Daughters of Destiny via

Facebook:
Raelyn Purham
DaughtersOfDestiny4YG
Instagram:
@iRockOriginality
@DaughtersOfDestiny4YG
SnapChat:
@Raeshines

www.ingramcontent.com/pod-product-compliance
Lightning Source LLC
Chambersburg PA
CBHW071107090426
42737CB00013B/2524